Any Time TEMPTATIONS SERIES

Sanjeev

Soups, Salads
.... & ....
SANDWICHES

Any Time TEMPTATIONS SERIES

Sanjeev Kapoor's

Soups, Salads
.... & ....
SANDWICHES

In association with Alyona Kapoor

PopulaR
prakashan

POPULAR PRAKASHAN PVT. LTD.
35-C, Pt. Madan Mohan Malaviya Marg,
Tardeo, Mumbai - 40 034.

First Published 2002
First Reprint January 2003
Second Reprint March 2005

(3811)

ISBN - 81-7991-065-2

PRINTED IN INDIA
By Alert Packaging House Pvt. Ltd., 326, A to Z Industrial Estate
Lower Parel, Mumbai and Published by Ramdas Bhatkal
for Popular Prakashan Pvt. Ltd.
35-C, Pt. Madan Mohan Malaviya Marg,
Tardeo, Mumbai - 40 034.

Dedication

This book is dedicated to
all the viewers of Khana Khazana
and my family and friends
who have been a constant support
to me at all times.

Note to the Readers

Oh, give me a bowl of soup, a sandwich and a good book to read and I would be happy! This enchanting collection of nourishing soups and exotic salads together with sandwiches from different parts of the world make a harmonious blend. This book is a part of the series of 'Any Time Temptations'. All the recipes have been picked out from my earlier books and segregated. All time favourites like Hamburgers and Hot Dogs included in the contents of this book make it a 'must have' for one and all. Also the everyday Aloo Chaat and Tomato Soup, which once incorporated in daily menus, will never leave the list of family favourites.

Now let's get ready for some globe trotting! The only thing to take along is a whetted appetite. Let's begin with our *desi* Bombay Vegetable Sandwich. Travel straight to Italy with the beautiful Italian Bruschetta and Focaccia. And while the going's good, try out the Pita Sandwich even if it means a bit of travelling to the Middle East!

Zip off to the Orient for a Warm Thai Noodle and Papaya Salad. Better still, stay back in the Mediterranean for the full flavour of the Poached Fish and Dill Salad. It is a treat worth anything. As the choices become difficult, it is your decision making skills that will be put to the test. But why bother? Just succumb!

A good choice for those who count the calories could be between the Spinach and Tofu Soup and the Chicken Barley Soup. Those who love soup as a meal could count on the hearty and nutty Roasted Pumpkin and Walnut Soup. For the adventurous there is Mushroom Cappuccino. Well, the recipe is no secret but we might tell you there is certainly no coffee in this soup!

All the recipes serve four portions and form part of a menu.

For a choice of dressing up the dishes turn to the section of Sauces and Dressings but don't blame us if you find it difficult to tear yourself away! For me, the choice is clear: a nourishing soup, a chunky sandwich and a good book...what more can one ask for!

Acknowledgements

A. I. Kazi
Aditi Mehta
Afsheen Panjwani
Anand Bhandiwad
Anil Bhandari
Blue Cilantro, Mumbai
Brijesh Lohana
Capt. K. K. Lohana
Debasis Sikdar
Drs. Meena & Ram Prabhoo
Ganesh Pednekar
Grain of Salt, Kolkata
Harpal Singh Sokhi
Jaideep Chaubal
Jijesh Gangadharan
Jyotsna & Mayur Dvivedi
Lohana Khaandaan

Meghana Samant
Namrata & Sanjiv Bahl
Neelima Acharya
Neena Murdeshwar
Pooja & Rajeev Kapoor
Rajeev Matta
Rajneesh Sharma
Rutika Samtani
Shivani Ganesh
Smeeta Bhatkal
Sunit Purandare
Swapna Shinde
The Yellow Chilli, Jalandhar
The Yellow Chilli, Ludhiana
Tripta Bhagattjee
Uma Prabhu

CONTENTS

SPINACH
AND
TOFU SOUP

INGREDIENTS

Tofu (bean curd) .... 100 gms
Spinach .... 1 bunch
Ginger .... ½ inch piece
Garlic .... 2 cloves
Oil .... 1 tsp

Vegetable stock .... 3 cups
Light soy sauce .... 1 tbsp
Salt .... to taste
Pepper powder .... to taste

METHOD OF PREPARATION

1 Cut the tofu into one-fourth inch thick slices and then cut them into one inch triangles.
2 Wash the spinach leaves thoroughly under running water. Remove stems, roughly shred and keep them aside. Peel and chop ginger and garlic.

15

3   In a wok or frying pan, heat oil on high heat and sauté chopped ginger and garlic.
4   Add the vegetable stock and bring to a boil.
5   Add the tofu pieces and light soy sauce and when it comes to a boil reduce heat and simmer for about two minutes.
6   Add the shredded spinach leaves and simmer for a minute stirring gently. Remove the scum to make clear soup.
7   Add salt and pepper powder to taste and serve hot.

Note : Refer page no. 103 for the recipe of Vegetable Stock.

Spinach & Tofu Soup

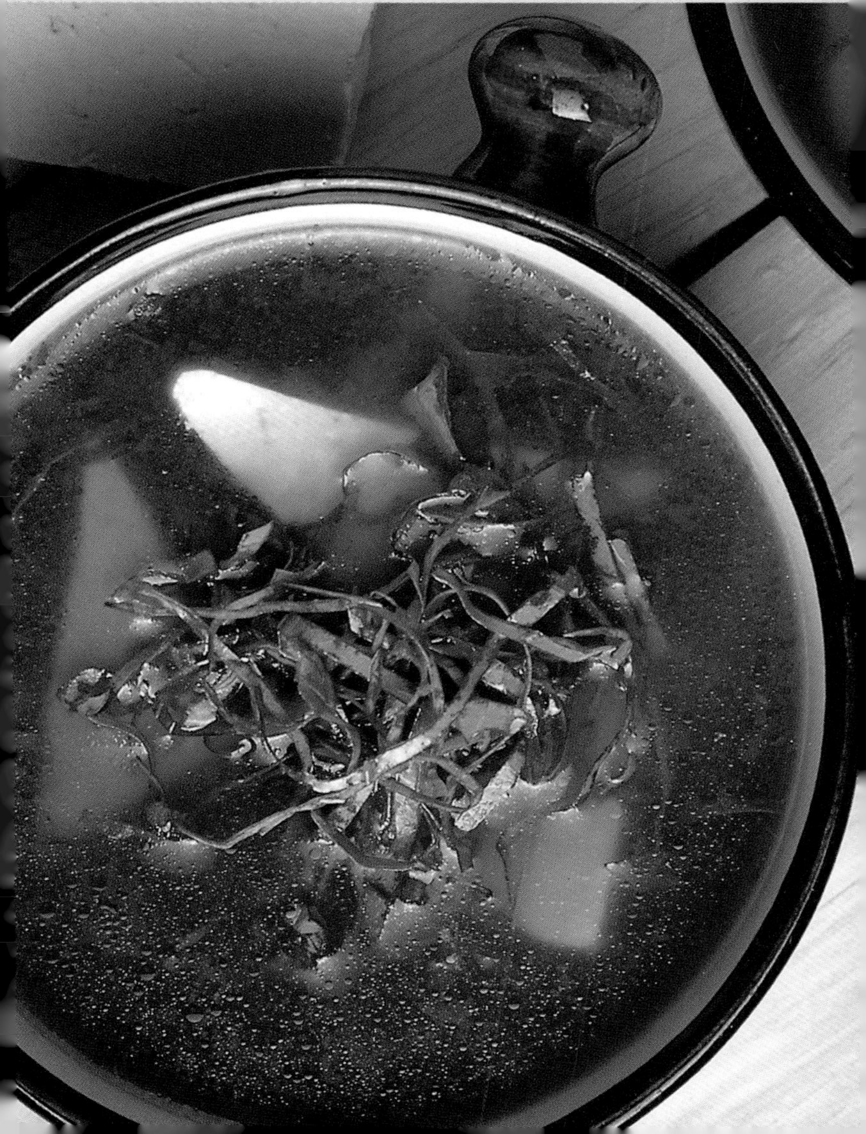

SAFFRON AND SEA FOOD SOUP

INGREDIENTS

Fish fillets	200 gms	Cream	½ cup
Prawns	8 small sized	Butter	1 tbsp
Spring onion	1	Salt	to taste
Fish stock	3 cups	White pepper powder	½ tsp
Saffron	a few strands	Lemon juice	1 tbsp
Egg	1	Parsley (chopped)	1 tbsp

METHOD OF PREPARATION

1 Clean, wash and cut fillets into half inch cubes. Remove shells, devein and wash the prawns. Wash and cut the spring onion bulb into thin slices. Wash and chop some spring onion greens for garnish.
2 Boil the fish stock with saffron strands reserving some strands for garnish.

3   Separate yolk of the egg and mix with cream.
4   In a pan melt the butter and toss in sliced spring onion.
5   Add the seafood and sauté for two to three minutes. Add the fish stock and bring to a boil. Simmer for around eight to ten minutes. Add salt, pepper powder and lemon juice.
6   Pour a ladle of soup in the cream and egg yolk liaison and mix. Put this mixture back into the soup.
7   Garnish with chopped parsley leaves, spring onion greens and the reserved saffron strands and serve hot.

Note : Refer page no. 104 for the recipe of Fish Stock.

MINESTRONE

INGREDIENTS

Carrot.................. 1 medium sized

Potato................. 1 medium sized

Zucchini .... 1 medium sized

Garlic .... 4-6 cloves

Onion .... 1 medium sized

Green peas (fresh) .... ¼ cup

Celery........................ 1 inch stalk

Leek .... ½ stalk

French beans 3-4

Fresh basil leaves 10-12

Tomatoes .... 4 medium sized

Oil .... 1½ tbsps

Vegetable stock .... 4 cups

Macaroni .... 2 tbsps

Salt .... to taste

White pepper powder .... ½ tsp

Parmesan cheese (optional, grated)
.... ½ cup

METHOD OF PREPARATION

1 Peel, wash and cut carrot, potato and zucchini into one-centimeter cubes. Peel, wash and chop garlic and onion. Wash the green peas.

2 Wash and cut celery and leek into one-centimeter sized pieces.

String, wash and cut French beans into one-centimeter sized pieces. Wash and cut half of basil leaves into strips and keep in cold water.

3 Cut the base of the tomatoes and give a cross cut with a sharp knife on the top, just superficially. Boil some water in a pan, put tomatoes in it for ten to twenty seconds and transfer immediately into a bowl of cold water. Peel the skin with hand, cut into halves, remove seeds and cut further into one-centimeter sized pieces.

4 Heat oil (preferably olive oil) in a pan, add garlic, onion and carrot and sauté till onions are translucent. Add leeks and celery and stir-fry for a minute.

5 Add French beans, zucchini, potatoes, green peas and tomatoes. Add remaining half of the fresh basil leaves broken by hand. Sauté for a couple of minutes and add vegetable stock and bring it to a boil.

6 Add the pasta (macaroni) and boil further on high heat for five to seven minutes. Season with salt and white pepper powder.

7   Serve hot, garnished with fresh basil strips and grated parmesan cheese.

Note: Refer page no. 103 for the recipe of Vegetable Stock.

TOASTED ALMOND SOUP

INGREDIENTS

Almonds 20-25
Carrot .... 1 medium sized
Onion .... 1 medium sized
Butter .... 1½ tbsps
Cloves 5-6

White sauce .... 1 cup
Milk .... 2 cups
Fresh cream .... ½ cup
Salt .... to taste
White pepper powder .... ¼ tsp

METHOD OF PREPARATION

1 Soak almonds in warm water for half an hour. Peel them and keep aside.
2 Slice half of the almonds into fine slivers and toast in an oven or *tawa* until golden brown.
3 Peel, wash and chop carrot and onion.
4 Heat butter in a pan, add cloves, onion and carrot and sauté till

translucent. Add the remaining half of the almonds. Stir-fry for few minutes.

3   Add one cup of water and boil for five minutes.

4   Strain and make a puree of solids (vegetables and almonds).

5   Dilute the white sauce with milk or water and mix it with the puree. Put in a pan and heat. Bring it to a boil, reduce heat, add cream and simmer for five minutes. Adjust seasoning with salt and pepper powder.

6   Garnish the soup with sliced toasted almonds and serve hot.

Note: Refer page no. 99 for the recipe of White Sauce.

ROASTED PUMPKIN AND WALNUT SOUP

INGREDIENTS

Red pumpkin .... 700 gms
Walnuts kernels 8
Onion .... 1 large sized
Parsley .... 2 sprigs
Oil .... 1 tbsp
Butter .... 2 tbsps

Vegetable stock or water ...... 4 cups
Curry powder .... 1 tsp
Fresh cream .... ½ cup
Salt .... to taste
White pepper powder .... ¼ tsp
Lemon juice .... 1 tbsp

METHOD OF PREPARATION

1   Let pumpkin remain as one large piece (if whole, cut into two).
    Remove seeds, clean and wash it. Break the walnut kernels roughly.
2   Peel, wash and finely chop the onion. Wash and finely chop parsley.

25

3   Apply oil on the pumpkin and roast in preheated oven at 200°C for half an hour. Alternately sauté after peeling and cutting into small pieces along with the onion as described below.

4   Heat butter in a pan and add the chopped onions and sauté till translucent.

5   Remove the roasted pumpkin from the oven and allow it to cool. Peel and cut into cubes.

6   Add this and walnuts to the onion and add half of the stock or water, cook for five minutes. Take off the heat, cool and puree it.

7   Add to it the remaining stock or water. Put it back on heat, add curry powder and bring to a boil. Reduce heat, add cream and simmer briefly.

8   Season with salt, pepper powder and lemon juice. Serve garnished with chopped parsley.

Note : Refer page no. 103 for the recipe of Vegetable Stock.

MINTED GREEN PEAS SOUP

INGREDIENTS

Green peas (shelled) .... 1 cup
Onion .... 1 small sized
Garlic .... 2-3 cloves
Potato ....1 small
Fresh mint leaves 10-12
Butter .... 1 tbsp

Vegetable stock .... 3 cups
Milk .... 1 cup
Salt .... to taste
White pepper powder .... ¼ tsp
Cream ....½ cup

METHOD OF PREPARATION

1 Peel and wash onion and garlic and chop them fine. Peel and wash potato and cut into slices. Wash the mint leaves and green peas.

2 Heat butter in a pan, add onion and garlic and sauté for a while.

3 When the onion turns translucent add vegetable stock, potato slices and the mint leaves reserving a few leaves for garnish. Once the

liquid starts boiling add the green peas. Boil for five to seven minutes, without covering, on high heat.

4   When done remove from the heat, cool and strain. Reserve the stock for adding later. Puree the peas and other vegetables using a little stock, if required.

5   Mix puree of peas with the required amount of reserved stock and milk and heat it again. Add salt and white pepper powder.

6   Do not overcook. Finish with cream and serve garnished with the remaining mint leaves.

Note: Refer page no. 103 for the recipe of Vegetable Stock.

MUSHROOM CAPPUCCINO

INGREDIENTS

Mushrooms	15 large sized	Salt	to taste
Onion	1 small sized	White pepper powder	¼ tsp
Garlic	4-6 cloves	Cream	¾ cup
Butter	1 tbsp	Milk (chilled)	2 cups
Bayleaf	1	Cinnamon powder	1 tsp
Vegetable stock	4 cups		

METHOD OF PREPARATION

1 Clean, wash and thickly slice mushrooms. Peel, wash and finely chop onion and garlic.
2 Melt butter in a heavy bottom pan, add bayleaf, onion and garlic and sauté for two to three minutes or till onion becomes translucent.
3 Add mushrooms and sauté for a minute. Add one cup of vegetable

stock and cook for five more minutes. Remove from heat and cool. Remove bayleaf.

4 Make puree of the cooked mushrooms. Add the remaining vegetable stock to it.

5 Return to heat and bring it to a boil, add salt and white pepper powder and simmer the soup for two to three minutes.

6 Add the cream and remove from heat. Place soup in individual cups.

7 In a chilled bowl take the chilled milk and beat it with a fork. This will develop froth in it which can be collected with a ladle and placed on the hot mushroom soup giving it a cappuccino effect. Sprinkle cinnamon powder and serve.

Note: Refer page no. 103 for the recipe of Vegetable Stock.

HOT AND
SOUR
VEGETABLE SOUP

INGREDIENTS

Onion	1 medium sized	French beans	4-6
Carrot	½ medium sized	Cornstarch	2 tbsps
Ginger	1 inch piece	Oil	2 tbsps
Garlic	2-3 cloves	White pepper powder	½ tsp
Cabbage	¼ small sized	Salt	to taste
Celery	2 inch stalk	Sugar	½ tsp
Spring onion (greens only)	1	Ajinomoto	½ tsp
Button mushrooms	2	Soy sauce	2 tbsps
Bamboo shoot slice	1 medium sized	Green chilli sauce	2 tbsps
Capsicum	½ medium sized	Vegetable stock	4-5 cups
		Vinegar	2 tbsps

METHOD OF PREPARATION

1 Peel, wash and finely chop onion, carrot, ginger and garlic. Wash and finely chop the cabbage, celery, spring onion and mushrooms.

2 Boil the bamboo shoot slice in a little water for three to four minutes. Drain all the water away. Cool and finely chop.

3 Wash, halve, de-seed and finely chop the capsicum. Wash, string and finely chop the French beans. Dissolve the cornstarch in quarter cup of water and keep aside.

4 Heat oil in a wok or a saucepan, add the chopped onion, ginger, garlic and stir-fry briefly. Add the chopped celery, carrot, cabbage, bamboo shoot, mushroom, capsicum and French beans.

5 Cook the vegetables stirring continuously for two to three minutes. Add pepper powder, salt, sugar, ajinomoto, soy sauce, green chilli sauce and mix well.

6 Pour in the vegetable stock and bring to boil. Reduce the heat and simmer for three to four minutes. Gradually mix in the dissolved cornstarch and continue to cook till the soup reaches

the required consistency.
7 Mix in the vinegar and serve piping hot garnished with chopped spring onion leaves.

Note : Refer page no. 103 for the recipe of Vegetable Stock.

TOM YUM KUNG SOUP

INGREDIENTS

Prawns .... 20-30 small
Mushrooms 5-6
Fresh coriander leaves ..... 2 tbsps
Green or fresh red chillies.........4
Lemon grass .... 2 stems

Lime leaves................................... 6
Salt .... to taste
Fish sauce .... 2 tbsps
Red curry paste .... 1 tsp
Lemon juice .... 2-3 tbsps

METHOD OF PREPARATION

1 Clean, wash and slice the mushrooms. Clean, wash and chop the coriander leaves. Remove stems and wash the green chillies or fresh red chillies. Wash the lemon grass and lime leaves.
2 Remove the head and shells of the prawns and wash. Devein prawns and wash them thoroughly under running water.
3 Place the head and shells in a pan with four to five cups of water.

Bruise lemon grass stems, two lime leaves and two green chillies in a mortar or tear them with hand and add to the pan.

4 Heat the pan and bring the mixture to a boil, add salt, cover and simmer for fifteen minutes. Take off the heat and strain.

5 Slice the remaining chillies into fine roundels and reserve for garnish.

6 Heat the strained stock and bring to a boil. Add the sliced mushrooms and prawns and simmer for two to three minutes or until the prawns are pink and cooked.

7 Stir in the fish sauce, red curry paste and lemon juice to make the soup sharp and tangy. Adjust the seasoning.

8 Pour into a serving bowl and garnish with green or fresh red chilli roundels and the whole lime leaves. Serve piping hot immediately.

CHEF'S TIP
Add coconut milk to make it a little mild.

CHICKEN
BARLEY
SOUP

INGREDIENTS

Chicken legs (with bones and skin) 2

Carrots .... 2 medium sized

Barley .... ½ cup

Onion .... 1 medium sized

Celery .... 3 inch stalk

Cucumber .... 1 small sized

Parsley .... 1 tbsp

Cornstarch .... ½ tbsp

Bayleaf 1

Peppercorns 4-6

Butter .... 2 tbsps

Salt .... to taste

White pepper powder .... ¼ tsp

METHOD OF PREPARATION

1   Prepare chicken by washing it well, taking care that the skin is intact.

Peel, wash and cut carrots into one-inch sized batons. Soak barley in two cups of water for an hour.

2 Peel, wash and slice onion. Wash and cut celery into one-inch sized pieces. Wash, de-seed and cut cucumber into one-centimeter sized cubes. Wash and chop parsley.

3 Dissolve cornstarch in half a cup of water.

4 Take seven cups of water in a heavy bottom pan, add bay leaf, peppercorns, carrots, onion, celery and chicken to it.

5 Boil on medium heat, removing the scum from time to time. Cook for around half an hour on medium heat.

6 Strain the stock and keep it aside. Take chicken pieces, de-skin and dice the meat. Discard the vegetables.

7 Drain water from the soaked barley.

8 Melt butter in another pan on low heat, add barley and cook for three to four minutes.

9 Add the reserved stock and continue cooking for another half an hour. Season with salt and pepper. Add cooked and diced meat to the barley mixture and simmer for another three to four minutes.

Add dissolved cornstarch, cook for a minute and remove from heat. Add chopped parsley and stir.

10 Serve piping hot, garnished with cubes of cucumber.

TOMATO SOUP

INGREDIENTS

Tomatoes ... 10-12 medium sized
Garlic .... 4 cloves
Carrot .... ½ medium sized
Celery .... 2 inch stalk
Onion .... 1 medium sized
Parsley .... a few sprigs
Bread slices 2
Cream .... ¼ cup

Sugar .... 1 tsp
Oil .... ½ tbsp
Butter .... 1 tbsp
Bay leaf 1
Peppercorns 4-6
Salt .... to taste
Peppercorns (crushed) ...... ½ tsp

METHOD OF PREPARATION

1   Wash and cut tomatoes into quarters. Peel, wash and chop garlic. Peel, wash and cut carrots into roundels. Wash and finely chop celery. Peel, wash and slice onion. Wash and chop parsley.

2   Cut the bread slices into cubes and toast them in an oven or frying pan to make croutons.

3   Mix cream and sugar gently.

4   Heat oil and butter in a pan, add bay leaf, peppercorns, sliced onions and sauté until translucent. Add the chopped garlic and celery, stir-fry briefly.

5   Add carrot roundels and tomatoes, stir-fry for a minute and add three cups of water. Bring it to a boil.

6   Cook for ten to fifteen minutes covered with a lid. Strain the blended mixture through a strainer. Reserve the liquid. Remove peppercorns and bay leaf from the residue and allow it to cool. Blend in a mixer to get a smooth puree. Pass it through a sieve or strainer.

7   Add the reserved liquid to the pureed tomatoes and adjust the consistency. Put it back on heat.

8   Add salt, freshly crushed peppercorns and let it simmer for a couple of minutes.

9   Before serving stir in cream and sugar mixture. Serve hot, garnished with parsley and toasted croutons.

TOMATO EGG DROP SOUP

INGREDIENTS

Tomatoes .... 4 medium sized
Eggs 2
Onion .... ½ medium sized
Ginger .... 1 inch piece
Garlic .... 2-3 cloves
Fresh coriander leaves ..... 2 tbsps
Cornstarch .... 2 tbsps

Vegetable stock or water .. 4 cups
Oil .... 2 tbsps
Tomato sauce .... 4 tbsps
Salt .... to taste
White pepper powder .... ½ tsp
White vinegar .... 1 tbsp

METHOD OF PREPARATION

1   Wash and finely chop tomatoes. Peel and finely chop onion, ginger and garlic. Wash, trim and finely chop coriander leaves.

2   Break eggs in a bowl and beat lightly. Dissolve cornstarch in a quarter cup of vegetable stock/water.

3   Heat oil in a saucepan, add chopped ginger and garlic and stir-fry briefly. Add chopped onion and continue to cook until the onion is translucent.

4   Add tomato sauce, chopped tomatoes and cook on high heat for about two to three minutes.

5   Add stock or water, salt to taste and white pepper powder. Stir and bring to a boil.

6   Gradually add the dissolved cornstarch, little at a time stirring continuously till the soup thickens to the required consistency. Add white vinegar and stir well.

7   Pour the beaten egg in a steady thin stream, stirring all the while to form egg strings. Allow the egg to coagulate and come to the top.

8   Serve hot garnished with chopped coriander leaves.

Note: Refer page no. 103 for the recipe of Vegetable Stock.

SWEET CORN VEGETABLE SOUP

INGREDIENTS

Sweet corn (cream style) .. 150 gms
Carrot .... ½ medium sized
French beans 4-5
Cauliflower .... ¼ medium sized
Cabbage .... ¼ medium sized
Cornstarch .... 2 tbsps

Vegetable stock .... 4½ cups
Salt .... to taste
White pepper powder .... ¼ tsp
Sugar .... ½ tbsp
Ajinomoto (optional) .... ¼ tsp

METHOD OF PREPARATION

1 Peel carrot and string French beans. Wash and finely chop all the vegetables. Parboil all the vegetables, drain and keep aside.
2 Dissolve cornstarch in a quarter cup of water and keep aside.

3 In a saucepan add the vegetable stock and bring to a boil.
4 Mix in the sweet corn and continue cooking till uniformly mixed.
5 Add salt, white pepper powder, sugar and ajinomoto. Gradually stir in the dissolved cornstarch into the soup, stirring continuously. After it comes to a boil cook for one more minute.
6 Now add the boiled vegetables and give a final boil and remove. Serve piping hot.

Note: Refer page no. 103 for the recipe of Vegetable Stock.

Sweet Corn Vegetable Soup and Vegetable Noodle Soup

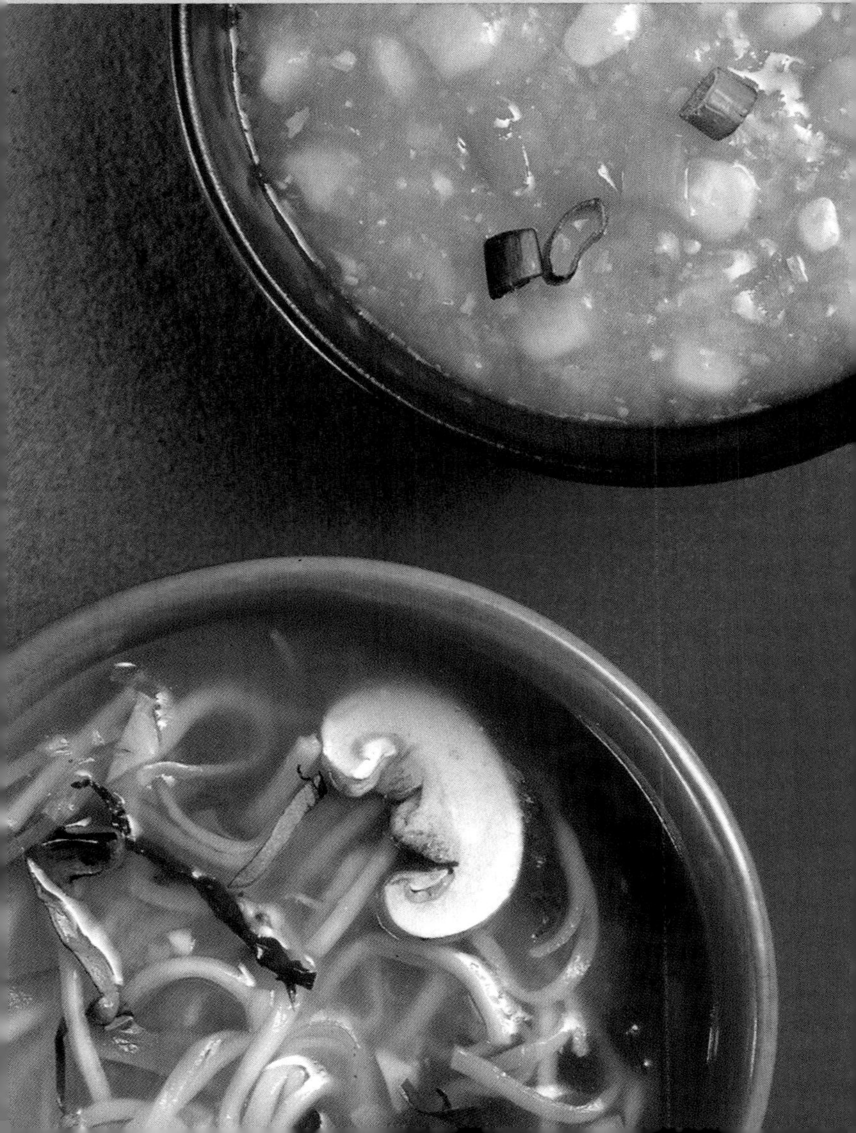

VEGETABLE NOODLE SOUP

INGREDIENTS

Mushrooms 4-5
Carrot .... 1 medium sized
Spinach .... 8-10 leaves
Capsicum .... ½ medium sized
Garlic .... 2-3 cloves
Red chilli whole 1
Oil .... 1 tbsp

Vegetable stock .... 4-5 cups
Noodles .... 40 gms
Ajinomoto .... ¼ tsp
White pepper powder .... ¼ tsp
Salt .... to taste
Vinegar .... 1 tbsp

METHOD OF PREPARATION

1 Clean, wash, trim and finely slice mushrooms. Peel, wash and cut carrot into julienne.

2 Wash, trim and finely shred spinach leaves. Wash, deseed and cut capsicum into julienne.

3 Peel and crush garlic. Wash, remove stem, deseed and shred whole

red chilli.
4 Heat oil in a wok or a pan, add crushed garlic and stir fry briefly.
   Add mushrooms, carrot, capsicum and stir fry for two minutes.
   Add shredded red chilli and immediately stir in stock.
5 Bring to a boil, add noodles, reduce heat and simmer for three to
   four minutes stirring occasionally.
6 Add ajinomoto, white pepper powder and salt to taste. Stir in vinegar
   and shredded spinach leaves, simmer for a minute and serve hot.

Note : Refer page no. 103 for the recipe of Vegetable Stock.

ALOO
CHAAT

INGREDIENTS

Potatoes	2 large sized	Lemon juice	1½ tbsps
Sweet potato	1 large sized	Salt	to taste
Fresh coriander leaves	½ bunch	Banana (ripe)	1 large
Green chillies	2	Tamarind pulp	2 tbsps
Ginger	1 inch piece	*Chaat masala*	1 tsp

METHOD OF PREPARATION

1   Wash and boil potatoes and sweet potato in sufficient water till cooked. Cool and peel.

2   Wash, trim and finely chop coriander leaves. Wash, remove stem and finely chop the green chillies.

3   Peel, cut ginger into thin strips, add half a teaspoon of lemon juice and a pinch of salt to it, keep in the refrigerator.

4   Cut potatoes and sweet potatoes into one inch sized cubes. Peel and cut banana into one inch sized pieces, apply half a teaspoon of lemon juice and keep aside.

5   In a mixing bowl take potatoes, sweet potatoes and bananas. Add the remaining lemon juice, tamarind pulp, green chillies, *chaat masala*, salt, chopped coriander leaves and toss lightly.

6   Serve garnished with ginger julienne.

CAESAR'S SALAD

INGREDIENTS

Bread ....2 thick slices	**For the dressing**	
Garlic ....2 cloves	Eggs 2	
Oil.. 1 tbsp	French mustard paste .... 1 tsp	
Lettuce leaves (iceberg) .... ½ bunch	Worcestershire sauce .... 1 tsp	
Lettuce leaves (lollorosso)... ½ bunch	Extra virgin olive oil .... 2 tbsps	
Basil leaves 5-6	Peppercorns (crushed) .... ¼ tsp	
Parmesan cheese .... 100 gms	Salt .... to taste	

METHOD OF PREPARATION

1 Cut the bread slices into one inch sized pieces. Peel and roughly crush garlic.

2 Heat oil in a pan and add garlic. Add the bread cubes and sauté till bread pieces are a little crisp and browned at the edges. Remove and keep aside.

3   Heat sufficient water in a pan, bring it to boil, add eggs and boil them for two to three minutes only.
4   Wash and tear the lettuce leaves and keep them in a big bowl. Tear the basil leaves and add to the lettuce. Add bread pieces with the garlic and toss lightly. Make cheese shavings using a peeler and add to the bowl or else grate the cheese.
5   Break the lightly boiled eggs into another bowl and whisk well. Add mustard paste, Worcestershire sauce, olive oil, salt and freshly crushed peppercorns and whisk till well blended.
6   Add dressing to the salad and toss lightly. Serve immediately.

CHEF'S TIP

You may come across different versions of Caesar's Salad in various hotels and restaurants. This is my favourite and was served in my friend's restaurant in Wellington, New Zealand.

PENNE IN THOUSAND ISLAND

INGREDIENTS

Penne (tubular pasta) .... 1 cup

Oil .... 1 tbsp

Capsicum .... ½ medium sized

Onion .... 1 medium sized

Carrot .... 1 medium sized

Broccoli .... ¼ small sized

French beans 3-4

Cherry tomatoes 10-12

Stuffed olives 4-5

Thousand Island Dressing ... ½ cup

METHOD OF PREPARATION

1   Take sufficient water in a pan, add a little salt and bring it to a boil. Add penne pasta and cook for six to eight minutes on high heat or until almost cooked. Drain, remove and refresh penne with cold water. Mix in one tablespoon of oil and spread on a plate.

2   Wash, de-seed and cut capsicum into one inch sized triangular pieces.
    Peel, wash, cut onion into quarters and separate the layers. Peel,
    wash and cut carrot into one inch sized pieces.
3   Wash and cut broccoli into small florets. String, wash and cut French
    beans diagonally into one inch sized pieces. Wash cherry tomatoes.
4   Heat sufficient water in a pan, add carrot, broccoli and French beans.
    Cook on medium heat for three to four minutes. Remove and refresh
    with cold water and drain of excess moisture.
5   In a large salad bowl toss all the prepared vegetables along with
    pasta, cherry tomatoes and stuffed olives.
6   Add Thousand Island Dressing, lightly toss and serve cold.

Note: Refer page no. 96 for the recipe of Thousand Island Dressing.

CHEF'S TIP

In case of non-
availability of
cherry tomatoes,
use normal
tomatoes cut in to
half inch sized
pieces.

GRILLED CHICKEN AND OLIVE SALAD

INGREDIENTS

Chicken breasts 2
Green olives 5-6
Black olives 5-6
Stuffed olives 5-6
Lettuce leaves ...... 1 small bunch
Oil .... 1 tbsp
Salt .... to taste
Peppercorns (crushed) .... ¼ tsp

Dressing
Rosemary .... 1 sprig
Fresh basil leaves 3-4
Thyme .... 2 sprigs
Olive oil .... 4 tsps
Lemon juice .... 2 tsps
Salt .... to taste
White pepper powder .... ¼ tsp
Sugar .... ¼ tsp

METHOD OF PREPARATION

1　Wash, de-skin and clean chicken. Pat dry with an absorbent kitchen towel.
2　Wash and finely chop the fresh herbs. Wash lettuce and tear them

Grilled Chicken & Olive Salad

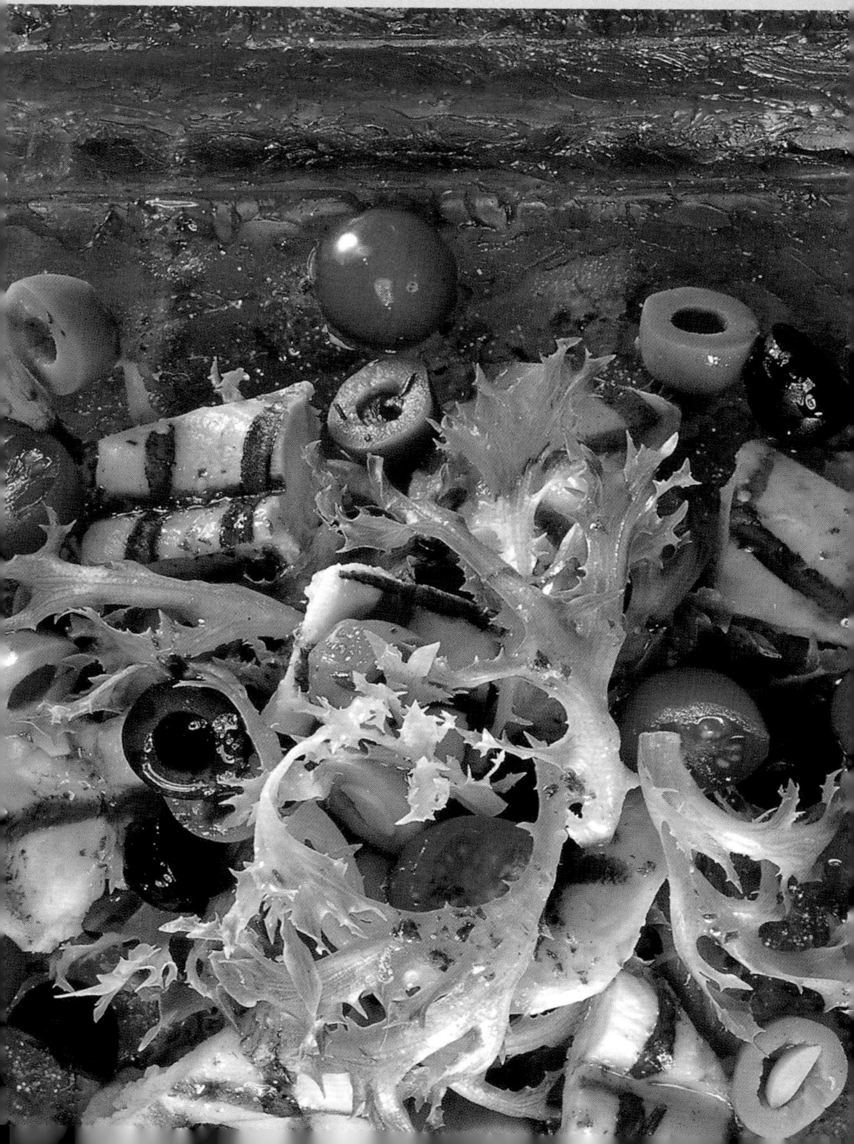

into bite sized pieces.

3 Marinate chicken breast in oil, salt, pepper and half a teaspoon of the chopped fresh herbs. Keep it in the refrigerator for an hour.

4 Mix olive oil, lemon juice, salt to taste, pepper, sugar and the remaining finely chopped fresh herbs to prepare the dressing.

5 Grill the chicken breast in a pre-heated grill or on a *tawa* on medium heat for eight to ten minutes or until done, turning once or twice, taking care that it remains juicy. Allow it to cool and cut into one inch sized pieces.

6 Add olives, lettuce leaves and the dressing. Toss lightly and serve immediately.

WARM THAI NOODLE AND PAPAYA SALAD

INGREDIENTS

Cellophane or glass noodles .... 100 gms

Raw papaya ...... ½ medium sized

Celery .... 1 stalk

Fresh coriander leaves ... a few sprigs

Garlic .... 4 cloves

Capsicum .... ½ medium sized

Peanuts (roasted) .... ½ cup

Oil .... 3 tbsps

Fish sauce (optional) ...... 2 tbsps

Salt .... to taste

White pepper powder .... ¼ tsp

Bean sprouts .... 1 cup

Lemon juice .... 1 tbsp

METHOD OF PREPARATION

1 Soak the noodles in hot water for a few minutes. Drain, refresh and add one-tablespoon oil. Mix well.

2   Wash, peel, remove seeds, clean and cut raw papaya into long and very thin slices. Wash, trim and slice the celery stalk. Wash, trim and chop coriander leaves.

3   Peel and chop the garlic. Wash, halve, deseed and cut the capsicum into half inch sized pieces. Crush the roasted peanuts.

4   Heat remaining oil in the pan. Add the garlic and stir-fry briefly or until light golden in colour. Add papaya slices, capsicum, celery and stir-fry for a minute.

5   Add the noodles and toss. Season with the fish sauce, salt and pepper powder. Remove from heat. Add crushed roasted peanuts and bean sprouts. Add lemon juice, mix well and serve warm, garnished with the coriander leaves.

Note: Fish Sauce is one of the most important ingredients in Thai and Oriental cooking. It is a mixture of anchovy (fish) extract and sea salt. It is readily available in the market in a bottle like most other sauces.

SUNSHINE SALAD

INGREDIENTS

Macaroni	¾ cup	Onion	1 medium sized
Oil	1 tbsp	Lettuce	1 medium bunch
French beans	5-6	Mayonnaise	2 tbsps
Corn kernels	½ cup	Salt	to taste
Red capsicum	½ medium sized	Red chilli flakes	1 tsp
Celery	1 stalk	Peppercorns (crushed)	¼ tsp

METHOD OF PREPARATION

1   Heat sufficient water in a pan. Bring it to a boil, add macaroni and cook for seven to eight minutes or until just done. Add oil, mix well, drain and remove. Refresh with cold water. Drain away the excess water.

2   Wash, string and cook French beans in salted boiling water for three minutes. Remove and refresh with cold water. Drain and cut the

beans into thin diamond shaped pieces.

3 Boil corn kernels in salted water for eight to ten minutes. Drain and keep aside.

4 Wash and cut red capsicum into thin strips. Wash and slice the celery. Peel, wash and finely chop onion. Wash and shred the lettuce leaves.

5 In a large salad bowl, mix macaroni with French beans, capsicum, onions, celery and corn kernels.

6 Chill until required. Mix in the mayonnaise, season with salt, red chilli flakes and crushed peppercorns.

7 Serve on a bed of shredded lettuce.

Note: Refer page no. 102 for the recipe of Mayonnaise.

POACHED FISH
AND
DILL SALAD

INGREDIENTS

Fish fillets	250 gms	Capsicum	1 medium sized
Fresh dill leaves	a few sprigs	Lemon juice	1 tbsp
Celery	2 inch stalk	Salt	to taste
Peppercorns	4-5	Peppercorns (crushed)	¼ tsp
Bayleaf	1	Olive oil	2 tbsps

METHOD OF PREPARATION

1 Cut fish fillets into one inch sized pieces. Wash and roughly chop dill leaves. Do not over handle the dill leaves. Wash and roughly slice the celery.
2 Heat sufficient water in a shallow pan, add peppercorns, bay leaf

and sliced celery. Bring it to a boil.

3   Add fish pieces and cook uncovered for two minutes or till the fish is done. Do not overcook. Remove from the water carefully and cool.

4   Wash, halve, deseed and cut capsicum into half inch sized diamond shaped pieces. Prepare dressing using lemon juice, salt to taste, crushed peppercorns and olive oil, add dill leaves to this dressing, reserving some for the garnish.

5   In a bowl arrange poached fish cubes carefully. Add capsicum pieces and sprinkle dressing. Gently mix and serve chilled garnished with the remaining dill leaves.

THREE CHILLI POTATO SALAD

INGREDIENTS

Baby potatoes	16-18	Sugar	1 tsp
Oil	1 tbsp	Salt	to taste
Green chillies	2-3	Red chilli flakes	2 tsps
Fresh coriander leaves	4 tbsps	Green peppercorns	1 tbsp
Lemon juice	2 tbsps	Tomato ketchup	1 tbsp

METHOD OF PREPARATION

1 Preheat the oven to 180°C. Scrub and wash baby potatoes well, prick with a fork, apply oil. Roast the potatoes in the preheated oven for thirty to forty minutes or till done.

2 Remove stem, wash, de-seed and chop the green chillies. Wash coriander leaves thoroughly and finely chop.

3 Cut the potatoes in halves when done with skin still on.

4   In a bowl take the lemon juice, sugar, salt, red chilli flakes, green chillies, green peppercorns and tomato ketchup. Mix well.

5   Add the potatoes and toss. Serve the salad garnished with chopped coriander leaves.

CHEF'S TIP

Use freshly crushed peppercorns as a substitute for green peppercorns.

PINEAPPLE WALDORF

INGREDIENTS

Pineapple slices	3	Mayonnaise	3 tbsps
Walnut kernels	½ cup	Cream	2 tbsps
Celery	1 stalk	Salt	to taste
Lettuce	1 bunch	Peppercorns (crushed)	½ tsp

METHOD OF PREPARATION

1   Cut pineapple slices into half inch sized pieces.
2   Toast the walnut kernels in an oven or on a *tawa* till a little crisp. Roughly break the walnuts into smaller pieces. Using a rolling pin crush a few walnuts to a coarse powder.
3   Wash, trim and cut celery stalk into half inch sized pieces. Thoroughly wash lettuce leaves and tear them into bite sized pieces.
4   In a mixing bowl, mix in pineapple, lettuce leaves and toasted

walnuts. Add mayonnaise and cream.

5 Add salt to taste and freshly crushed pepper. Lightly toss the salad so that the dressing evenly coats the pineapple, walnut and lettuce leaves.

6 Garnish it with coarse walnut powder and serve cold.

Note: Refer page no. 102 for the recipe of Mayonnaise.

CROISSANT CHICKEN SANDWICH

INGREDIENTS

Croissants 4

Chicken breasts (boneless) 2

Fresh mint leaves ..... a few sprigs

Fresh coriander leaves ... a few sprigs

Onion .... 1 medium sized

Capsicum .... ½ medium sized

Tomato ketchup .... 4 tbsps

Coriander and Mint Chutney ....
.... 2 tbsps. + to serve

Salt .... to taste

Chaat masala .... 1 tsp

Butter/mayonnaise .... 2 tbsps

Lettuce leaves 4

METHOD OF PREPARATION

1   Boil chicken and cut into one-centimeter strips. Wash the mint leaves and place in chilled water. Wash and chop coriander leaves.

2   Peel, wash and chop onion. Wash, de-seed and chop capsicum.

3   In a bowl mix together chicken strips with tomato ketchup, onion, capsicum, coriander leaves, two tablespoons of Coriander and Mint Chutney and sprinkle salt and *chaat masala*. Divide this mixture into four.

4   Remove mint leaves from chilled water. Pat them dry.

5   Cut the croissants into half and toast on a *tawa*/griddle. Apply butter or mayonnaise.

6   Arrange the lettuce leaf on one half of the croissant. Spread one portion of the chicken mixture on it followed by mint leaves. Cover with the other half and repeat this process with the remaining croissants. Serve with tomato ketchup or Coriander and Mint Chutney.

Note: Refer page no. 101 for the recipe of Coriander and Mint Chutney and page no. 102 for the recipe of Mayonnaise.

VEGETABLE CLUB SANDWICH

INGREDIENTS

Bread	12 slices	Pineapple slices	2
Carrot	1 medium sized	Mayonnaise	¼ cup
Capsicum	1 medium sized	Butter	4 tbsps
Cabbage	¼ medium sized	Cheese slices	4
Lettuce	½ bunch	Salt	to taste
Tomatoes	2 medium sized	White pepper powder	¼ tsp
Cucumber	1 medium sized		

METHOD OF PREPARATION

1 Toast the bread slices. Peel, wash and grate carrot. Wash, halve, de-seed and cut capsicum into thin strips. Wash and grate the cabbage. Wash lettuce and pat dry.

2 Wash and cut tomatoes into slices. Peel, wash and cut cucumber

into slices. Cut pineapple into small pieces.

3 Mix mayonnaise with capsicum, carrot and cabbage to make coleslaw. Add pineapple pieces to it. Season well.

4 Apply butter on all the toasted bread slices on one side and on both the sides of four of them. Place four slices of bread, single side buttered, on a board. Arrange half of the lettuce leaves on them, keep some coleslaw aside for serving as accompaniment and spread the remaining evenly on all the four slices. Arrange another layer of bread slices, both sides buttered, on it. On this bread slice place the remaining lettuce leaves, tomato and cucumber slices, sprinkle seasoning and place cheese slices.

5 Cover with the final layer of toasted bread slices, single side buttered. Lightly press with palm to set the ingredients well.

6 Using a very sharp knife cut the edges of the sandwich and cut it diagonally. Serve with coleslaw and potato wafers.

Note: Refer page no. 102 for the recipe of Mayonnaise.

CHEF'S TIP

One can also make Tomato omelet or Fried egg and place in between as one of the stuffings of the sandwich.

73

BOMBAY
VEGETABLE
SANDWICH

INGREDIENTS

Bread .... 8 slices	Butter .... 2 tbsps
Onions .... 2 medium sized	Coriander and Mint Chutney .... ½ cup
Cucumber 1	*Chaat masala* .... ½ tsp
Tomatoes .... 2 medium sized	Salt .... to taste
Potatoes .... 2 medium sized	Peppercorns (crushed) .... ½ tsp

METHOD OF PREPARATION

1   Peel, wash and cut onions and cucumber into roundels. Wash and cut tomatoes into roundels.
2   Wash and boil the potatoes. Allow them to cool. Peel and slice.
3   Trim the sides of the bread slices, apply butter and Coriander and Mint Chutney.

4   On a flat board, arrange four bread slices with chutney spread, layer it with onion, cucumber, tomato roundels and potato slices. Sprinkle some *chaat masala*, salt and crushed peppercorns. Cover each of them with another slice of bread and press it lightly.

5   Cut each sandwich into six equal portions and serve it with tomato ketchup.

Note: Refer page no. 101 for the recipe of Coriander and Mint Chutney.

BRUSCHETTA

INGREDIENTS

Hard crust bread .... 1 loaf	Basil leaves 5-6
Garlic .... 8-10 cloves	Olive oil .... 1 tbsp
Butter .... 4 tbsps	Salt .... to taste
Tomatoes .... 3 large sized	Peppercorns (crushed) .... ¼ tsp

METHOD OF PREPARATION

1   Cut the bread loaf diagonally into half-inch thick slices. Peel and finely chop the garlic. Mix half of it with butter and spread well on the slices. Toast the slices in the oven till crisp.

2   Wash, halve, de-seed and finely chop tomatoes. Wash and cut basil leaves into strips. Save some for garnish.

3   In a bowl mix together chopped tomatoes, basil strips, olive oil, remaining half of the garlic, salt and crushed peppercorns. Rest the mixture for about half an hour.

4   Spread the mixture over the toasted garlic bread pieces and serve garnished with strips of basil.

PIN
WHEEL
SANDWICH

INGREDIENTS

Fresh bread loaf (whole) 1

Mayonnaise .... ¼ cup

Tomato ketchup .... ½ cup

Red chillies (crushed) .... 1 tsp

Salt .... to taste

White pepper powder .... ¼ tsp

Butter .... 4 tbsps

METHOD OF PREPARATION

1 Cut the fresh bread loaf lengthwise in a sheet form. Trim off the crusts.

2 Mix tomato ketchup, mayonnaise, crushed red chillies, salt and white pepper powder.

3 Apply butter on one side of the bread.

4   Spread the filling on the buttered side evenly. Roll the bread slowly taking care not to break it. Wrap in a greaseproof paper and place in the refrigerator to set for thirty to forty-five minutes.
5   When set, remove the paper from the roll, cut into two-centimeter thick slices, arrange neatly on a platter and serve.

VARIATION FOR SPREADS

1   Mix mayonnaise, chopped lettuce (five-six leaves), grated cheese (half a cup), salt and white pepper powder.
2   Jam or marmalade.
3   Coriander and mint chutney.

Note: Refer page no. 102 for the recipe of Mayonnaise.

GRILLED
KALKA
SANDWICH

INGREDIENTS

Left-over cooked vegetable (pre ferably dry) .... 1 cup
Fresh coriander leaves ...... ¼ cup
Bread .... 8 slices

Butter .... 4 tbsps
Lemon juice .... 1 tsp
Chaat masala .... ½ tsp

METHOD OF PREPARATION

1   Clean, wash and finely chop the coriander leaves. Butter the bread slices using half of the butter.

2   Mix the left over vegetable well and mash, if required. If the vegetable is with gravy, cook it on high heat to remove excess moisture.

3   Mix lemon juice, chopped coriander and *chaat masala* with the vegetable mixture. Divide into four.
4   Place the vegetable mixture on four of the buttered bread slices. Cover with the remaining bread slices and toast in a sandwich toaster on either side, applying the remaining butter to the exposed side of the bread slices. Remove when golden brown.
5   Serve hot with Coriander and Mint Chutney or tomato ketchup.

VARIATIONS

1   *Dal* stuffing: It can be first sautéed in butter with chopped onions and tomatoes and then used as stuffing.
2   *Rajma* stuffing: Normally *rajma*, when kept in the refrigerator overnight becomes thick and dry. If not, then drain the gravy, mash the *rajmas* and reheat with some of the drained gravy for the desired consistency.
3   Chicken stuffing: If dry boneless chicken dish is leftover then it

can be shredded and used but if curried chicken is left, then the chicken pieces should be removed, de-boned, shredded and then stuffed.

Note: Refer page no. 102 for the recipe of Coriander and Mint Chutney.

CHEF'S TIP

Grilled Kalka Sandwich has nothing to do with Kalka station near Simla. It's actually KAL-KA (yesterday's) but if you present it as Kal Ka or yesterday's, nobody would touch it, would they?

GRILLED VEGETABLE AND CHEESE SANDWICH

INGREDIENTS

Bread .... 8 slices
Potatoes .... 2 medium sized
Capsicum .... 1 medium sized
Onion .... 1 large sized
Tomatoes .... 2 medium sized
Butter .... 4 tbsps

Coriander & Mint Chutney .... 4 tbsps
Cheese (grated) .... ½ cup
Salt .... to taste
Pepper powder .... ¼ tsp
Chaat masala .... 1 tsp

METHOD OF PREPARATION

1   Boil, peel and grate potatoes. Wash, de-seed and chop capsicum. Mix grated potatoes and chopped capsicum.
2   Peel, wash and thinly slice onion. Wash and slice tomatoes.

3   Apply butter and Coriander and Mint Chutney on one side of all the bread slices.

4   Place four slices of bread on a board and spread a layer of potato and capsicum mix on each slice evenly.

5   Place onion and tomato slices and cheese on it. Sprinkle salt, pepper and *chaat masala*. Finally, cover it with the remaining slices of bread. Lightly press so that all the layers are firm and even.

6   Preheat the sandwich grill. Apply butter on the exposed side of the bread slices and grill for five minutes or till golden and crisp from both sides.

7   Cut the grilled sandwich with a sharp knife and serve with tomato ketchup and Coriander and Mint Chutney.

Note: Refer page no. 101 for the recipe of Coriander and Mint Chutney.

PITA SANDWICH

INGREDIENTS

Pita bread 4
Chicken breasts (boneless) 2
Tomatoes .... 2 medium sized
Capsicum .... 1 medium sized
Onion .... 1 medium sized
Lettuce .... 1 bunch
Pickled jalapenos (optional) 4

Oil .... 2 tbsps
Salt .... to taste
Peppercorns (crushed) .... ¼ tsp
Cucumber .... 1 medium sized
Yogurt .... ¼ cup
Cream .... ¼ cup

METHOD OF PREPARATION

1   Clean, wash and pat dry the chicken breasts, cut into three-centimeter long strips. Wash and cut tomatoes into roundels.
2   Wash, halve, deseed and cut capsicum into julienne. Peel, wash and slice onions. Wash and roughly chop the lettuce. Cut jalapeno into slices.

3   Heat oil in a pan, add onion slices and sauté. When the onions become translucent add chicken and capsicum. Sauté till the chicken is cooked, season with salt and crushed peppercorns. Remove and keep aside.

4   Peel, wash, halve, deseed and finely chop the cucumber, beat yogurt well with cream. Combine the two and season.

5   Cut open the side of pita bread to make pockets. Stuff in a layer of shredded lettuce, slices of tomatoes, jalapenos, a large spoonful of cucumber-yogurt relish and the chicken and capsicum mix. Top with another layer of shredded lettuce. Serve with a dip of your choice.

Pita Sandwich and Focaccia with Chicken & Mozzarella

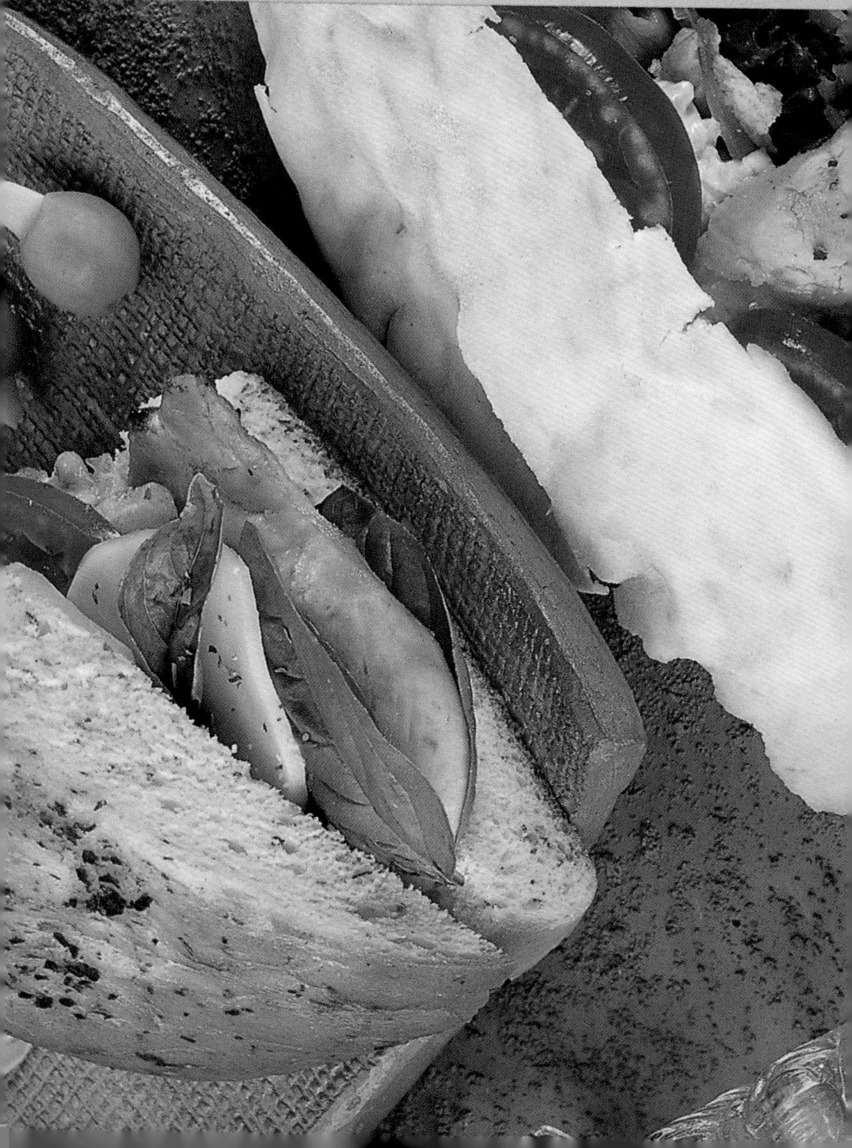

FOCACCIA WITH CHICKEN AND MOZZARELLA

INGREDIENTS

Focaccia bread (6 inch diameter) 4
Fresh basil leaves 8-10
Mozzarella cheese............. 50 gms
Fresh parsley leaves .. a few sprigs
Chicken breasts (boneless) 2

Tomatoes .... 2 medium sized
Olive oil (preferably extra virgin)
.... ¼ cup
Salt .... to taste
Peppercorns (crushed) .... ¼ tsp

METHOD OF PREPARATION

1   Slice each focaccia bread horizontally into two. Wash and pat dry the fresh basil leaves.

2   Slice cheese into four slices. Wash and chop parsley. Clean and wash chicken breasts and pat dry. Slice each chicken breast into two.

3   Wash and cut tomatoes into half-centimeter thick slices. Make a marinade of olive oil, parsley, salt and pepper powder.

4   Keep one-fourth of marinade aside. Marinate the cheese slices and chicken breasts, separately in the remaining marinade for an hour.

5   Heat a grill or *tawa*. Pick the chicken breasts from the marinade and cook them over the grill/*tawa*, covered, till both sides are done.

6   Apply remaining marinade to the foccacia bread slices. Place the basil leaves on the base along with the tomato slices and marinated mozzarella cheese slice. Place a piece of grilled chicken breast and cover with the another slice of focaccia and serve.

CHEF'S TIP

Focaccia is a herb flatbread from Italy. It has become a popular alternative to ordinary sliced bread. It is flatter and drier in texture than the familiar fresh white loaf from the bakery, and is made in large squares or rounds as well as in small rounds like flattened bread rolls.

JUNGLI CHICKEN

INGREDIENTS

Chicken breast (boneless) 1	Lettuce .... ½ bunch
Bread .... 8 slices	Mayonnaise .... ¼ cup
Capsicum .... 1 medium sized	Salt .... to taste
Green chillies 2	White pepper powder .... ¼ tsp
Onion .... 1 medium sized	Cheese (grated) .... ½ cup
Cabbage .... ¼ small sized	Butter .... 4 tbsps

METHOD OF PREPARATION

1   Wash, halve, de-seed and chop capsicum. Wash, remove stem, de-seed and finely chop green chillies. Peel, wash and chop the onion. Wash, remove stalk and grate cabbage.

2   Wash and clean chicken, boil it in sufficient water till cooked and allow it to cool. Cut into small pieces. Wash, pat dry lettuce and roughly shred it.

3   Mix chicken and all the vegetables (except lettuce) with mayonnaise, add chopped green chillies, adjust the seasoning with salt and pepper. Mix in grated cheese.

4   Butter the bread slices. Divide the mixture into four equal portions. Place half of the shredded lettuce on four of the buttered bread slices, spread chicken and vegetable mixture evenly on the bread. Place the remaining lettuce and cover with the remaining buttered slices.

5   Slightly press the sandwich. Trim the edges, using a sharp knife and cut diagonally before serving.

Note: Refer page no. 102 for the recipe of Mayonnaise.

HAMBURGER

INGREDIENTS

Burger buns.................................. 4
Mutton mince .... 400 gms
Onions................ 2 medium sized
Cucumber .... 1 medium sized
Tomatoes .... 2 medium sized
Lettuce leaf..................... 1 bunch
Bread crumbs (optional).. ½ cup
Peppercorns (crushed) .... ½ tsp

Egg.. 1
Mayonnaise .... 4 tbsps
Tomato ketchup .... 2 tbsps
Mustard paste...................... 1 tbsp
Salt .... to taste
Oil .... 3 tbsps
Butter .... 2 tbsps
French fries .... as required

METHOD OF PREPARATION

1   Peel, wash and slice the onions and cucumber, wash and slice the tomatoes. Clean, wash, shred and keep the lettuce leaves in ice water for some time to retain its freshness.

2   In a medium-sized mixing bowl, combine the mutton mince, breadcrumbs, salt, half of the crushed peppercorns and egg together.

3   Mix mayonnaise with tomato ketchup, mustard paste and season with salt and remaining pepper.

4   Divide the mince mixture in four balls and flatten them to form a thick pattie. Keep the mixture in the refrigerator for half an hour. The size of the pattie should be larger than the size of the bun in diameter as it will shrink on cooking.

5   Heat oil in a non-stick pan or *tawa* and shallow fry the mutton patties, till they are golden brown, on both sides.

6   Slit the burger buns in half, apply butter on each half and toast on a *tawa* or grill. Remove and place on a working top.

7   Apply mayonnaise mix to the shredded lettuce. Place the lettuce leaves on the base-half of the burger and over it place cucumber and tomato slices. Now place the mutton pattie and finally a slice of onion. Put the other half of the bun and close. Repeat the process with the remaining buns.

8   Secure with wooden sticks across so that the pattie is held within.

9   Serve hot accompanied with French fries.

Note: Refer page no. 102 for the recipe of Mayonnaise.

> **CHEF'S TIP**
>
> Vegetarians can replace the mutton patties with potato or paneer patties.

93

HOT DOG

INGREDIENTS

Hot dog buns...............................4
Chicken sausages 4
Lettuce ....1 bunch
Onions................ 2 medium sized

Butter .... 2 tbsps
Tomato ketchup .... 4 tbsps
Mustard paste (optional)... 2 tbsps

METHOD OF PREPARATION

1 Slit the hot dog buns into half without cutting it into two. Heat a *tawa*. Roast the inside of the buns on it for a minute.
2 Wash and shred the lettuce. Peel, wash and chop the onions.
3 Take a pan, add butter and sauté the chicken sausages till cooked and golden brown.
4 Apply butter on the inside of the buns, apply tomato ketchup and arrange the shredded lettuce. Place chopped onion and then the hot sausages.
5 Spread the mustard paste and serve hot.

CHEF'S TIP

Vegetarians can replace sausages with Aloo Paneer Rolls.

VINAIGRETTE DRESSING

INGREDIENTS

Vinegar	4 tbsps	Salt	to taste
Olive oil or salad oil	12 tbsps	White pepper powder	½ tsp
Dijon mustard	1 tsp	Sugar	1 tsp

METHOD OF PREPARATION

1 Whisk all the ingredients together in a bowl. Always shake before using as oil and vinegar tend to settle separately. It has a shelf life of one week if stored in a refrigerator.

VARIATIONS

1 Garlic Vinaigrette: Add two to three chopped cloves of garlic to the recipe.
2 Herb Vinaigrette: Few leaves of coriander or mint can be used after washing and finely chopping.
3 Tomato Vinaigrette: Two tablespoons of tomato ketchup can be added to the mixture and whisked.

CHEF'S TIP

This is one way of making Vinaigrette. You can alter the ratio of vinegar and oil and make variations. Lemon juice can be an alternative to vinegar, if desired. Vinegar quality too would determine the final outcome.

95

THOUSAND ISLAND DRESSING

INGREDIENTS

Spring onion 1

Red capsicum .... ¼ small

Stuffed olives 5-6

Egg 1

Mayonnaise .... 4 tbsps

Tomato ketchup .... 2½ tbsps

Tobasco sauce .... 1 tsp

Salt .... to taste

White pepper powder .... ¼ tsp

METHOD OF PREPARATION

1   Wash, peel and finely chop the bulb of the spring onion. Wash, halve, de-seed and chop the red capsicum. Remove stuffed olives from the brine, wash and cut into small pieces.

2   Boil egg for ten to twelve minutes in boiling salted water, drain, cool, shell and chop.

3   In a bowl, mix mayonnaise with tomato ketchup, chopped olives, spring onion, red capsicum, half of the chopped boiled egg and tobasco sauce.

4   Add salt and white pepper and mix well. Chill in the refrigerator.

ORANGE HONEY
DRESSING

INGREDIENTS

Lemon juice .... 2 tbsps
Orange juice .... 4 tbsps
Honey .... 2 tbsps
Basil (fresh) .... 3-4 leaves

Olive/vegetable oil .... ¼ cup
Salt .... to taste
Red chilli powder .... ½ tsp
Lemon rind (grated) .... ½ tsp

METHOD OF PREPARATION

1   Wash and cut basil leaves into fine strips.
2   Mix both the citrus juices in a bowl, add honey, olive oil and mix
    well.
3   Season with salt, red chilli powder, basil strips and lemon rind. Mix
    well.

WHITE SAUCE

INGREDIENTS

Refined flour (*maida*) ... 1½ tbsps
Butter .... 2 tbsps
Onion .... 1 medium sized
Bayleaf 1
Cloves 2

Milk .... 1½ cups
Nutmeg .... a small pinch
Salt .... to taste
White pepper powder .... ¼ tsp

METHOD OF PREPARATION

1 Melt one and half tablespoons of butter in a thick-bottomed pan.
2 Add the flour, stir and cook the roux (butter-flour mixture) over low heat with a wooden spoon. When it gets the sandy texture remove from the heat and cool.
3 Peel onion. Wrap a bayleaf around it studding it with cloves at two ends.
4 Bring the milk to boil with the studded onion. Remove the onion.
5 Pour the boiling hot milk into the cold roux stirring continuously

to avoid lumps. Simmer gently for two minutes. Add seasoning and nutmeg.
6   Melt the remaining butter and layer the top of the sauce with it to avoid formation of skin.

VARIATIONS

1   Cream sauce: Add one-fourth cup of cream and two tablespoons of melted butter to the ready white sauce and mix.
2   Parsley: Add one tablespoon of chopped parsley to the cream sauce and mix.

CORIANDER AND MINT CHUTNEY

INGREDIENTS

Fresh coriander leaves .... 1 cup
Fresh mint leaves .... ½ cup
Green chillies 2-3

Black salt .... to taste
Sugar .... ¼ tsp
Lemon juice .... 1 tsp

METHOD OF PREPARATION

1 Clean, wash and roughly chop the coriander and mint leaves.
2 Remove stem, wash, de-seed and chop the green chillies.
3 In a mixer, process chopped coriander and mint leaves with chopped green chillies. Make a smooth paste using a little water if required and remove. Add salt and sugar.
4 Remove in a bowl and mix in the lemon juice.

VARIATION

Add yogurt to the chutney and mix properly (one cup of yogurt for two tablespoons of chutney).

CHEF'S TIP

To add sourness you can use crushed dry pomegranate seeds or dry mango powder (*amchur*) instead of yogurt and lemon juice. In season raw mango is a good substitute.

MAYONNAISE

INGREDIENTS

Egg yolk 1	Sugar .... ¼ tsp
Salt .... to taste	Vinegar .... 1 tsp
White pepper powder .... ¼ tsp	Oil .... 1 cup
French mustard powder ..... ¼ tsp	Lemon juice .... 1 tsp

METHOD OF PREPARATION

1   Take a clean bowl. Place egg yolk, salt, white pepper powder, mustard powder, sugar and vinegar in it and mix it thoroughly with a whisk or hand or else transfer to a blender.

2   Add oil, a little at a time, whisking/blending continuously, until all the oil is incorporated.

3   Finish the sauce by adding lemon juice and adjust the seasoning.

CHEF'S TIP

Vegetarians can replace sausages with Aloo Paneer Rolls.

VEGETABLE STOCK

INGREDIENTS

Onion	1 medium sized	Bayleaf	1
Carrot	½ medium sized	Peppercorns	5-6
Celery	2-3 inch stalk	Cloves	2-3
Garlic	2 cloves		

METHOD OF PREPARATION

1   Peel, wash and slice onion and carrot. Wash and cut celery into small pieces. Peel and crush garlic.
2   Take all the ingredients in a pan with five cups of water and bring it to a boil.
3   Simmer for fifteen minutes and strain. Cool and store in a refrigerator till further use.

FISH STOCK

INGREDIENTS

Fish bones, head, skin .. 200 gms
Onion .... 1 medium sized
Celery .... 2-3 inch stalk

Mushroom .... 1 large
Bay leaf 1
Peppercorns 4-6

METHOD OF PREPARATION

1   Peel, wash and slice onion, wash and cut celery into one centimeter pieces, wash and slice mushroom.

2   In a pan put fish bones, head, skin (any unutilised portion of fish), five cups of water, onion slices, mushroom slices, celery pieces, bayleaf and peppercorns and put it on heat.

3   Bring it to boil, remove any scum, which comes on top and then simmer for fifteen minutes. Remove from heat, strain and use the liquid as stock.

CHEF'S TIP

Fish stock should not be stored in the refrigerator as it smells and affects other food.

Subscribe to www.sanjeevkapoor.com NOW

Subscribe now, get fabulous discounts! Have the benefit of saving and also enjoy free books!!

Access to more than 1000 recipes besides many other sections, which will be a rare culinary treat to any food lover. In addition to online contests, etc., you will also have opportunities to win fabulous prizes.

Sanjeev Kapoor also invites all food lovers to participate in the Khana Khazana quiz and win BIG prizes every week. Watch Khana Khazana on Zee TV, answer correctly, one simple question based on that day's episode, combine it with a favourite recipe of yours and you can be the lucky winner going places!

Type	One year Subscription to www.sanjeevkapoor.com	Sanjeev Kapoor's 3 Best Selling Books Absolutely free	Total worth	You pay (offer value)	You Save	Your Choice
Yellow Chilli	Rs.1000/-	Rs.750*	Rs.1750/-	Rs.750/- (US $ 13)+	Rs.1000/-	☐
Red Chilli	Rs.1000/-	....	Rs.1000/-	Rs.500/- (US $ 10)+	Rs.500/-	☐

* Conditions Apply
* For subscribers requesting delivery of the free books within India an additional sum of Rs.50 (Rupees Fifty only) will be levied as delivery charges.
* For subscribers requesting delivery outside India, additional Rs.500/- delivery charges will be levied for airmail charges on the Yellow Chilli offer.
\+ Foreign exchange rates are approximate.

HURRY!!! OFFER OPEN TO FIRST 1000 SUBSCRIBERS ONLY

Choose your three free books with the Yellow Chilli subscription

Khazana of Indian Recipes	Khazana of Healthy Tasty Recipes	Khana Khazana —Celebration of Indian Cooking	Low Calorie Vegetarian Cookbook	Any Time Temptations	Best of Chinese Cooking	Microwave Cooking Made Easy	Simply Indian
MRP: Rs 250	MRP: Rs 250	MRP: Rs 250	MRP: Rs 250	MRP: Rs 225	MRP: Rs 250	MRP: Rs 250	MRP: Rs 250
☐	☐	☐	☐	☐	☐	☐	☐

I'm enclosing Cheque/DD No. _____ dated _____ for Rs._____ (in words)
_____ on (specify bank and branch) _____
favouring Popular Prakashan Pvt Ltd, Mumbai

For Credit Cards

Charge Card ☐ VISA ☐ Master Card for Rs. _____

Credit Card No. ☐☐☐☐☐☐☐☐☐☐☐☐☐☐☐☐

Card Expiry Date ☐☐ ☐☐ Card Member's Date Birth ☐☐ ☐☐ ☐☐☐☐
             MM   YY   DD MM   YYYY

Card Member's Name _____

For ☐ Yellow Chilli Subscription ☐ Red Chilli Subscription

Name: Mr./Ms _____
Address: _____
City: _____ Pin: _____ State: _____ Country: _____
Phone Res.: _____ Off.: _____ E-mail: _____
Please fill in the coupon in capital letters and mail it with your Cheque/DD to :

Popular Prakashan Pvt Ltd,
35-C, Pt. Madan Mohan Malaviya Marg, Tardeo, Mumbai - 400 034.
Phone: 022-24941656, 24944295, Fax : 022-24945294
E-mail : info@popularprakashan.com, Website : www.popularprakashan.com

*Delivery subject to realisation of Cheque/DD.
Please allow two weeks for processing your subscription. Please superscribe your name and address on the reverse of the Cheque/DD.
All disputes are subject to the exclusive jurisdiction of competent courts and forums in Mumbai (India) only.

This Coupon entitles the bearer redemption of Rs.50/- against purchase of Sanjeev Kapoor's books worth minimum Rs.100/-

Valid upto 31st December 2005

This Coupon entitles the bearer redemption of Rs.50/- against purchase of Sanjeev Kapoor's books worth minimum Rs.100/-

Valid upto 31st December 2005

This Coupon entitles the bearer redemption of Rs.100/- against purchase of Sanjeev Kapoor's books worth minimum Rs.300/-

Valid upto 31st December 2005

This Coupon entitles the bearer redemption of Rs.100/- against purchase of Sanjeev Kapoor's books worth minimum Rs.300/-

Valid upto 31st December 2005

For further enquiries contact:

Popular Prakashan Pvt. Ltd.
35-C, Pt. Madan Mohan Malaviya Marg, Tardeo, Mumbai-400 034
Phone: 91-22-24941656 Fax: 91-22-24945294
E-Mail: info@popularprakashan.com
Website: www.popularprakashan.com, www.sanjeevkapoor.com

TERMS AND CONDITIONS FOR REDEMPTION

1. This coupon can be redeemed against the purchase of Sanjeev Kapoor books by sending this coupon along with payment to Popular Prakashan.
2. The offer is valid as per the mentioned date.
3. The coupons are valid only against the printed MRPs and will not work with any other special offers or promotions at the time of purchase.
4. The coupons are non-transferable and non-encashable.
5. No two coupons can be clubbed together.
6. Each coupon is valid for one time purchase only.

Popular Prakashan Pvt. Ltd.
35-C, Pt. Madan Mohan Malaviya Marg, Tardeo, Mumbai-400 034
E-Mail: info@popularprakashan.com
Phone: 91-22-24941656 Fax: 91-22-24945294

TERMS AND CONDITIONS FOR REDEMPTION

1. This coupon can be redeemed against the purchase of Sanjeev Kapoor books by sending this coupon along with payment to Popular Prakashan.
2. The offer is valid as per the mentioned date.
3. The coupons are valid only against the printed MRPs and will not work with any other special offers or promotions at the time of purchase.
4. The coupons are non-transferable and non-encashable.
5. No two coupons can be clubbed together.
6. Each coupon is valid for one time purchase only.

Popular Prakashan Pvt. Ltd.
35-C, Pt. Madan Mohan Malaviya Marg, Tardeo, Mumbai-400 034
E-Mail: info@popularprakashan.com
Phone: 91-22-24941656 Fax: 91-22-24945294

TERMS AND CONDITIONS FOR REDEMPTION

1. This coupon can be redeemed against the purchase of Sanjeev Kapoor books by sending this coupon along with payment to Popular Prakashan.
2. The offer is valid as per the mentioned date.
3. The coupons are valid only against the printed MRPs and will not work with any other special offers or promotions at the time of purchase.
4. The coupons are non-transferable and non-encashable.
5. No two coupons can be clubbed together.
6. Each coupon is valid for one time purchase only.

Popular Prakashan Pvt. Ltd.
35-C, Pt. Madan Mohan Malaviya Marg, Tardeo, Mumbai-400 034
E-Mail: info@popularprakashan.com
Phone: 91-22-24941656 Fax: 91-22-24945294

TERMS AND CONDITIONS FOR REDEMPTION

1. This coupon can be redeemed against the purchase of Sanjeev Kapoor books by sending this coupon along with payment to Popular Prakashan.
2. The offer is valid as per the mentioned date.
3. The coupons are valid only against the printed MRPs and will not work with any other special offers or promotions at the time of purchase.
4. The coupons are non-transferable and non-encashable.
5. No two coupons can be clubbed together.
6. Each coupon is valid for one time purchase only.

Popular Prakashan Pvt. Ltd.
35-C, Pt. Madan Mohan Malaviya Marg, Tardeo, Mumbai-400 034
E-Mail: info@popularprakashan.com
Phone: 91-22-24941656 Fax: 91-22-24945294